This journal belongs to

____

The Universe knows what you need and is leading you towards it, even now.

THE RELEVANT, RESPECTFUL AND ESSENTIAL NATURE OF SHAMANIC HEALING FOR ALL

Shamanism is an ancient and multifaceted tradition arising within Indigenous cultures throughout the world. Each culture has its own nuanced understanding and techniques for practice, languaging and cosmic view incorporated into its shamanic wisdom, and yet there are meaningful, common threads to be found within shamanic teachings from a broad and diverse range of cultures. There is a profound core unity that reflects the importance of shamanism not only for various cultures, but for humanity as a whole. This underlying universal shamanistic wisdom is an expression of what it is to be human in the most wholistic sense—embracing our spiritual potential as human beings, our physical existence with its associated difficulties, and our place within the greater ecosystem of life, honouring our sacred relationships with all beings.

Within many human hearts, there is a great yearning to reconnect with this shamanistic wisdom and to heal through it, even if we do not always couch it in shamanic-oriented language. At the heart of such yearning is the need to feel connected to and a part of—rather than apart from—life.

Ancestral trauma arising from wounds of dislocation due to migration, war and colonialism is the karmic inheritance of the majority of human beings on the planet at this time. Many people want to find their own Indigenous heritage, and when those cultures are no longer in existence, or are in other ways inaccessible to the person, there can be a sense of feeling rootless and lost. Such hearts can heal through a more universal approach to shamanic wisdom, allowing them to attune themselves to legitimate lineages in an unconventional yet authentic and beneficial way.

Living shamanic culture—including the threads of authentic shamanic wisdom and practice that have woven their way into our broader collective culture—can help ground humanity. A more grounded humanity results in the maturation of human culture. We need this. The planet and her creatures need this. Such maturity results in more presence, an awareness of the impact of our actions in the environment and an increased ability to be spiritually fed by natural Earth and Sky energies.

When we are spiritually fed as a species, we are more able to fulfil our innate divine potential, radiating light, compassion, wisdom and love in action for the benefit of the greater good. We become sources of healing in our lives and in our world. Instead of reenacting the traumas of disconnection and loss, we can move through them, and co-create a sacred rebirth for humanity and our world. For this to happen, we must honour the deepest principle of shamanic wisdom—we are one, with each other, with our planet, with her precious creatures. We must work together. We must share our wisdoms and our medicines. We must seek to heal and love each other as best we can.

INTO YOUR SHAMANIC HEALING JOURNEY

As with all of my work, when you are drawn to this particular publication, it means something for you and your soul journey. It is a divine diagnostic of sorts. You could consider your spiritual attraction to this journal as a sign that your own shamanic healing journey is especially relevant for you at this time.

What that looks like for you may be different to how it shows up in the life of another person. However, there are certain elements of shamanic healing that are consistent and universal. An essential element of the shamanic path is a feeling that you must heal a certain issue or circumstance in your life. There is no viable alternative to this—it is a question of heal or perish. Those who are tackling their deepest wounds will understand this—healing feels like an issue of survival, as one simply cannot continue in the same suffering and struggle indefinitely.

Shamanic healing will lead you to a spiritual crossroads. This crossroads is a choice point. It asks that the shamanic soul accepts the symbolic death of the old identity, the old way of being, so that a new way can arise. For this to occur, we have to be willing to close the relevant karmic doors completely. We process our experiences and then put the past behind us. This is not token closure, it is a deep and complete release. It can be confronting. We are not only letting go of past experiences but our sense of self, stories and attachments wrapped up in those experiences. We may want to free ourselves and yet at the same time recognise the enormous courage required to do so.

> ***The shamanic soul has to make a decision — will I continue on in the same way that I have been, familiar as that has been, or will I dare to confront uncertainty with trust, and grow through my healing process with courage?***

Dying symbolically to the old self requires considerable, deep inner work. Being willing to come alive again as if spiritually reborn takes enormous energy, too. At the right moment, the shamanic soul will recognise that the threshold for spiritual rebirth is before them—the transitional point of initiation. There is no turning back. There is a new life within this lifetime to live as fully as we can. But we must cross that inner threshold and allow it to occur.

Shamanic healing becomes relevant for human beings when we are ready for it at a spiritual level. At a conscious intellectual level, you may not be so sure, but your soul knows what you need and what can benefit you in the truest and deepest sense, and evokes relevant situations and experiences to help you access what you need.

When shamanic healing feels meaningful to you—even if you aren't entirely sure why at a conscious level—then your soul is speaking to you. You are being called to a path of meaningful and likely even dramatic change, to become your truest self in a way that you probably don't yet consciously grasp. The shamanic healing process is the soul birthing process that will allow this spiritual transformation and rebirth to occur.

Regardless of where you sense yourself to be on this shamanic healing path—at the beginning, challenging depths, or crossing the threshold of rebirth even now, your heart knows what you need and how to guide you through it. It is wise to open your heart to the divine support that has sufficient strength to help you navigate the phases of the process and live the truth of your path. So much goodness and beauty arise from this. This journal has been created to help support you through shamanic healing in whatever way it is unfolding for you. The *Medicine Heart Oracle* has also been created to offer you more in-depth guidance and practices for your unique soul healing journey.

HOW TO HONOUR YOUR SHAMANIC HEALING PROCESS

Below is some universal guidance that can help you honour and facilitate your shamanic healing process, in whatever way that may be manifesting in your life.

The shamanic healing path requires courage.

What this means is that at times you will probably not want to take the steps that your heart guides you to take. Or you may want to, but question your ability to do so. Why would that occur? You may feel uncertain as to whether you have what it takes to embrace the unknown. It might feel like an uncomfortable leap of faith is being asked of you. In such cases, your intuition is likely way further ahead in awareness than your conscious mind. This can happen often. The result is that we feel inspired or guided to take a certain step, whilst our intellect may question or resist acting on it. Inner conflict arises and we might feel confused and stuck.

The truth is that even when we trust our intuition and make the best possible decision with the resources available to us in that moment, we will not necessarily know how things are going to unfold. Learning to be okay with uncertainty whilst still honouring your heart's guidance can be tough at first, and then very freeing as you realise that you are meant to be alive and take a soul journey, not control external events and outcomes. We can give our path our all, and then detach—like letting a bird leave the nest and fly free. Who knows what that bird will encounter mid-flight? Yet it has the courage and confidence to embrace the journey.

Perhaps the most powerful basis of courage is trust. This means trusting yourself, trusting your path and process, trusting your spiritual connection and trusting in the intelligence of life and the Universe that wants you to grow and awaken spiritually. How that unfolds is out of your control, but choosing to take the journey is entirely your own responsibility.

The shamanic healing path requires patience.

Sometimes we may resist the call to patience and opt for pushing instead. Patience doesn't mean that we become passive. We can still be doing all that we can in working towards the outcome we want, yet we also accept that there is wisdom in divine timing. The blade of grass doesn't grow faster by tugging at it. What it needs are the right conditions to encourage growth, and then the inner intelligence of that little blade—which belongs to the greater wisdom of the ecosystem of life—will do what it needs to do.

You and I are not so different to that blade of grass. Patience recognises this. It allows us to detach from the pressure to accomplish things on the schedule of our egos. Sometimes the ego thinks things should happen in a flash, or in a preferred order of events. Yet the soul knows that, like the seasons of Earth Mother, good things take time, and certain events need to happen before other events can occur. Even that which may appear as if it has happened suddenly will have had plenty of incubation time in the depths of the soul before complete manifestation and expression can arise. Soul timing is a wisdom that leads us towards fruition, and patience is key to allowing that wisdom to lead.

Patience is not holding us back or blocking us—it is a way for us to align with the greater wisdom of the cycles of life. Think of it like being carried by a wave to the shore, rather than paddling against the currents on your own. You cannot control when the wave arises, but you can prepare yourself to be able to work with it at the opportune moment. So patience is not only about slowing down at times, it's also about swifter movement at the right time, and preparation in the interim.

Divine timing is really a matter of alignment with the rhythms of our soul and of life, and so although the call to patience may evoke sighs of frustration, it can also be a welcome return to grounding and connection with the authentic self. There is actually so much goodness that happens for the soul when we embrace patience as a friend of our hearts.

The shamanic healing path requires flexibility and creativity.

Flexibility is the basis of creativity. When we are focused on accomplishing a certain outcome, Life will not always comply with our plans as to how and when that will manifest.

Taking a creative approach to your life means that you are willing to respond to what arises—even the unexpected—with a flexible attitude. A flexible and creative attitude is *responsive*. To cultivate a responsive attitude, we first do our best to clearly see what *is* (rather than how we may wish things to be). Then we can respond to that as we choose.

> ***When we choose to work with Life rather than routinely pushing against it, we can also choose to trust that there is benefit to be gained from our experiences. We don't have to lose heart or undermine our confidence to continue when things go awry. Given that life is askew and unpredictable much of the time, embracing a flexible and creative approach can ease our suffering. We can make the most out of whatever arises in the best way we can manage in that moment.***

Flexibility and creativity allow you to be guided by your own healing journey, rather than feeling happy or sad based on whether life meets your expectations. This shift in attitude and approach can be deeply healing. It allows us to experience our spiritual path as a co-creation with Life's wisdom and the healing journey as a wild, creative and very authentic expression of our own inner truth. In a society where we are told what to believe, and are often confounded by conflicting points of view and disinformation, returning to the truth of your heart and your soul journey can restore a sense of sanity, sacredness and satisfaction in your life.

The shamanic healing journey requires confidence.

Remember that you are inwardly ready for shamanic healing, or you wouldn't be attracted to this material. The divine timing and process will arise as suits you at a soul level. This is an expression of the spiritual wisdom of your soul and the kindness and generosity of the Universe in cooperation.

> ***You can trust how your path unfolds, when and with whom. The path will rarely be predictable, and yet in a reassuring way, you will know that you are doing your inner work and something good and gracious is growing because of that. That positive spiritual seed will eventually manifest as blessings in your inner and outer world.***

There may be chaos or uncertainty at times—when you are doing deep inner work such experiences are unavoidable. Yet your heart will be urging you on with a loving wisdom, recognising that the pain will pass and in its place will arise healing, relief and clarity—and the spiritual strength you need to fulfil your life path and purpose with greater joy.

Having confidence in your process — and affirming your ability to see things through—will inspire your bravery. You can also remember that your journey is entirely your own. There is guidance for you, and teachings to contemplate, but this is not an examination with a right or wrong answer. You are meant to be learning through your own experience. This is the growth that will facilitate your particular path and way to healing and renewal.

May you effortlessly recognise and attract all that your soul needs to fulfil its healing journey, expressing an inspired purpose and grounded path, living your heart's truth with compassionate wisdom.

Alana x

Every situation holds the secret divine potential to become a gift.
It is how we choose to work with a situation that matters most.
You can find a way to make every life circumstance serve your soul destiny.

Give yourself the divine downtime you need to process your experiences so you can settle your mind and heart in trust.

Let your heart be encircled by sacredness. There is every reason to hope for transformative beauty as you embrace the power of your healing journey.

SHAMANIC HEALING INFUSIONS WITH SEASONAL WISDOM MEDICINE

The four practices outlined in this journal are designed to inspire and support the shamanic facets of your soul-healing journey.

Every soul moves through a healing journey in its own unique way and according to divine timing. Your soul has an inner wisdom akin to the wisdom of Mother Earth, knowing when to retreat for restorative hibernation in spiritual winter, when to rally one's energies and arise for the spiritual spring, when to radiate with openness and confidence during the sacred summer of the soul, and when it is time to let go of what has been in order to start the cycle again.

These shamanic healing practices provide you with an accessible method to infuse your soul with the sacred seasonal wisdoms. These wisdoms are a type of sacred soul medicine—they strengthen the positive aspects of the season and help you transform any negative associations with each season into a constructive attitudinal energy your soul can utilise.

The integration of seasonal wisdom medicine empowers the shamanic transformational process. It can be disconcerting—to put it mildly—when, in the face of your best efforts, what matters most in your life may seem to be disintegrating before your eyes. To have trust that this is a clearing and release that will ultimately fertilise a new and more expansive cycle for you in the longer term can provide much-needed reassurance and boost one's courage to continue. It is not a disaster—your soul is just moving through winter in order to approach the rebirth of spring.

I have provided you with four key practices here—one that resonates with the essence of each of the four seasons in your soul healing journey. If you live or have travelled in a place where these seasons are pronounced, then you will likely be somewhat familiar with the energies, and it may just be a matter of learning to integrate seasonal energies at a subtle soul level. For others, it may be that certain seasons are different to your local environment. For you, there may be a process of exploring the qualities of seasonal changes that are not so familiar to you and allowing a new medicinal energy repertoire to awaken in your soul!

Unlike the shifting seasons on the physical level, at a soul level, seasons will have a much more fluid sense of timing. Perhaps you may feel as though you are in a seasonal phase for a long time—much longer than it would be in any given year in a physical sense. This can especially be the case with the spiritual winter when the soul is preparing for a truly expansive and abundant cycle ahead. There often needs to be much clearing and conservation of energies in preparation for this, so the autumnal clearing that happens prior to that winter may be particularly intense too. The spiritual autumn and winter may last for more than a few months each. Or they could be intense but far swifter. Your own soul timing is governed by a healing intelligence that you can trust. Then the spring and summer soul seasons that follow are often enriching in equal if not greater proportion. The deeper our roots can go, the higher our soul branches can reach.

Within these soul seasons, you will have seasonal mini-cycles. These may be days or hours where you dip into the seasonal medicine of autumn to help you release an attachment to something that is no longer meant to be in your life, or the summer where you need to find your confidence to shine bright, or winter, when you need some solitude and introversion to recharge your batteries — even if just for a day or two. You are a multidimensional being and it is entirely possible to experience cycles within cycles.

These seasonal practices can support you in the smaller and grander cycles of your spiritual journey and soul healing process. Trust your intuition and work with the practice that speaks to you at this time. It may be an intuitive inspiration that guides you, or you may simply want to align with the energy of the earth in her current seasonal expression wherever you are in the world at the time of practice. You cannot make a 'wrong' decision with your choice. Seasons flow into each other, strengthening the entire cycle. So whatever the method for your work, you can trust that the outcome will ultimately generate what is most needed.

The soul's healing journey may be gentle and nourishing at times, and at other times, may feel fierce, as though you are being transformed by a raging inner holy fire that demands complete, courageous surrender of who you once thought yourself to be, in order to become who you truly are! The nature of your healing journey at any given moment will reflect what is best and most beneficial for you. Sometimes that means we need to lay down to rest the anxieties that we have held on to for most of our lives, and grab hold of the hand of the divine instead. At other times, we may feel that we must find our courage to feel the fear and embrace the challenge anyway, rising beyond what we thought we were capable of, and giving ourselves permission to shine bright.

As you ground your connection to the earth and her wisdom medicines—such as seasonal teachings—you stabilise your energy and allow your spiritual channel to open to the Sky medicines of enlightened beings. To this end, I have included a simple enlightened guardian practice in each of the seasonal wisdom teachings too.

As you embrace the sacred spiritual medicines of Earth and Sky, your soul can function as the natural shamanic channel it is divinely designed to be. Your soul has the innate capacity to bridge heaven and earth, integrating and expressing multidimensional reality through your heart. As you embrace this shamanic soul capacity within you, self-healing and spiritual awakening instinctively occur. Having attained such spiritual integration, your heart organically functions as a wisdom keeper and light bearer. Your ability to radiate such beneficial consciousness will grow as you continue to heal, purify and awaken your heart. Shamanic practice can be an extremely effective way to do this, particularly when Earth medicines are partnered with Sky medicines of enlightened wisdom in your practice. Exploring your path of shamanic healing with integrity and commitment can generate profound personal fruition *and* collective benefit for our entire human family and our beloved Mother Earth.

Practical note: *You may wish to record the practices on your device and play it back for yourself. If you are using the practices for your personal use and not broadcasting or sharing them outside a private situation, you have the permission of the author and publisher to do so.*

You have it within you to respond constructively and creatively to anything and everything that is taking place in your life.

It is not until you fully embrace and lay claim to your right to exist —your right to live your life in integrity with your own heart— that the fulfilment of your destiny can unfold.

The sacred masculine energy within your soul has a higher purpose—
to create a positive legacy by honouring the heart with his powerful energy,
drive and inspired activity.

When something is destined to enter your life, it must happen. Events may arise creating a clearing so that the forthcoming grace has space to manifest.

There is a great source of spiritual power available to humanity. Access to such potency requires the willingness to abandon herd mentality, trust the heart and live life in alignment with deeper values of the soul and the spiritual laws of the Universe.

When facing a choice, consider the responses available to you.
What response would fill you with spiritual power?

A prayer to the Light

Beloved enlightened ones of unconditional love, divine healing and ageless wisdom, I call upon your protection and empowerment, and ask for blessings to accomplish my intention in such a way that generates spiritual benefit for all beings.

There is a way through a current dilemma that will open your heart to joy, but first, you may need to disengage from fear or doubt. Give yourself permission to determine what your own inner state of being shall be.

Your spiritual birthright is a sacred path to divine fruition.
Open your heart to the perennial reality of grace and guidance that exists for you,
ever warm and welcoming.

You are deeply connected to infinite sources of creative energy, love and healing. There is a difference between being strong and independent, and cutting oneself off from life-enhancing, heart-nourishing energies. Allow your exquisite human vulnerability and courage to attract spiritual grace.

From the raw material of fate, your soul has the power to craft divine destiny. You will be challenged, but the challenge is the method through which you shall attain fruition.

Believe in the beauty of what your heart is capable of attracting and manifesting as you continue to commit to your process.

Something good is destined to arise from all that is transpiring.

Honour the vulnerability inherent in your humanity and the heroism of choosing to be fully alive. Empower yourself to accept spiritual assistance whilst believing in your considerable capacity.

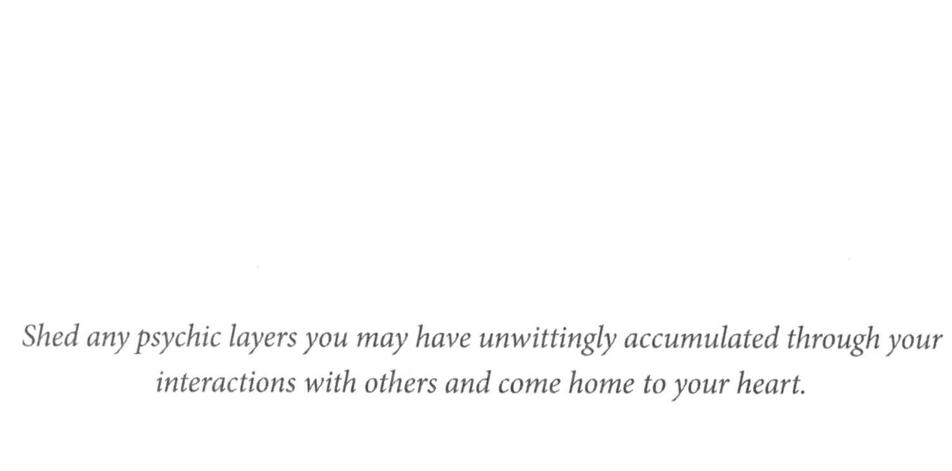

Shed any psychic layers you may have unwittingly accumulated through your interactions with others and come home to your heart.

There is a different view, a new energy or attitude arising within you. This may feel unfamiliar, yet it is trustworthy and grounded in goodness.

SACRED PRACTICE ONE – THE WISDOM OF WINTER

The Wisdom of Winter is a practice for when you need sacred introversion and intentional solitude to recharge your energy, replenish your heart, and reconnect to yourself and your truths. It supports the release of fixed patterns and unhelpful attachments, cleansing and returning your purified energy back to you.

Step One – Prepare the Space

How will you establish your sacred space? A simple candle, incense burning or altar could help you channel your focus into inner work, anchoring the intention to step beyond ordinary reality into the liminal spiritual energies that are with us always, but that we do not always notice amongst the distractions of daily life.

Colours that resonate well for winter are dark blue, black and white, but please be guided by your own sense of what you need. You may prefer to work with warmer colours that represent the hearthfire keeping you warm whilst the outer world is cloaked in darkness.

Step Two – Prepare Body and Mind

Ground yourself by becoming aware of your body—the weight of your body and the flow of your breath. Choose to be present. Connect to your heart in the way that suits you, perhaps by placing a hand at your heart and reflecting on that which evokes gratitude.

Allow that feeling of gratitude to awaken the energies within your heart. Imagine that the heart is shining with radiant pure love, in all directions. Relax and allow that love to wash through your being, cleansing your body and mind with peaceful, positive energy.

Step Three – Set Intention and Make a Dedication

Do you have a specific intention for the practice? Or are you simply open to what can be revealed through the practice? If you set a specific intention, maintain flexibility in your heart to embrace experiences that may change your way of seeing

your situation. Sometimes we discover that what we thought was the problem is only a symptom and there is a more effective way to manifest a solution.

When you are ready, you can dedicate the practice by declaring, "May spiritual benefit for all beings be authentically generated through this work." This dedication ensures that your practice amplifies the positive and will enhance the benefits of the practice for you and for others indirectly also.

Step Four – Cast the Medicine Circle

The medicine circle is the sacred space within which healing and energy work can safely unfold without distortion or disruption.

Visualise and/or feel that there is pure divine love, shining as a vibrant red jewel, glowing in your heart and sparkling with golden light. That jewel emanates golden-red light in all directions and through all dimensions, forming a subtle energy circle around you. This demarcates the sacred space.

Sense that at each of the four points of the circle—north, south, east and west—as well as above you and below you, there is a strong glowing golden light. This represents the enlightened guardians protecting the circle.

Step Five – Heart of the Practice

Imagine and intend that you are entering into the sacred space within your heart.

In the vastness of that open spaciousness within your heart, you can sense the depths of the night unfolding all around you, as if you are floating, yet secure, in the vast, empty spaciousness.

Here you can empty out all of the superfluous mental activity and emotional energy so that it can be purified and returned to you fresh and filled with creative potential. Anything and everything you wish to release will be received here and transformed.

If you wish to include a deity practice, you can now invoke the dark goddess of healing and protection, Kali, with this simple mantra, asking for her support and blessing for your process. As you sound the mantra, imagine all negativities, impurities or pain dissolving into nothingness and arising again as positive energies flowing back into you.

Jai Ma Kali Ja Ma Jai (sounds like JAY MAH KAR-LEE JAY MAH JAY)

Step Six – Return

Sense that your process is now complete and you are at the transitionary threshold, ready to return to this moment renewed.

Your inner shift may be radical or subtle but you are ready to step back into your life in a new way. Whatever has arisen for you is what is most needed in this moment. Trust your own soul process.

Step Seven – Closing and Grounding

Slowly move your hands into prayer position at your heart, intending to seal all that has transpired with love. Then say, "It is done."

Intend to bring your awareness completely into the present moment. Sense the air on your skin and the weight of your body in this world. The divine portal closes and all energies from the work dissolve into light and are released to where they can do the most good.

Intend to ground yourself fully in the present moment with some gentle movement.

You have completed your practice.

Change may feel startling, refreshing or even disruptive. It may be welcomed warmly or contemplated cautiously. Yet change can be a circuit breaker, providing an opportunity for creative evolution.

You are completely responsible for your life, your personhood and your voice. You can assert your light without dominating another. You can lead whilst remaining in humble service to the Universal Divine Heart.

Within the spiritual power centre of the throat chakra dwells your creative healing potency of voice, choice, vibration and resonance. Honouring the significance of your words and choices is the path to activating your creativity and spiritual channel.

Soon there will be a realisation that what has unfolded was a spiritual preparation period, and you are now perfectly equipped for expansion into a greater sphere of expression.

Your future will not be bound by the struggles you are grappling with.

You have the innate spiritual capacity to heal yourself, tame wild forces and generate light. This ability arises spontaneously as you practise consistently aligning yourself with the strength, wisdom and unconditional compassion of your heart.

As you tune in and allow for it, everything that you need to heal, awaken, make progress, and resolve a problem will come to you gracefully. Trust in the magnetic potency of your heart.

As you count your blessings, you will facilitate a shift from a fear-driven, grasping mind, into a grateful, magnetic and trusting heart.

Gather to you—with intention—that which nourishes, protects, inspires and supports you in claiming your innate connection to sacredness and the realms of spirit, healing, grace and protection. This shall strengthen your heart light, benefitting you and all beings.

You have more power to bring about positive healing change in your life than you may realise. Your life is in your own blessed hands.

Do not allow what has unfolded in the past to become the basis for the interpretation of the present moment or the expectation for your future. There is positive healing change now unfolding within you and good shall come of it.

Know that you are blessed with spiritual guides and soul guardians who are looking out for you. You will be gifted with the knowledge of what is true and what to do.

Earth Mother is inventive, resourceful and generous with her ample medicinal treasures. There is promise of a spiritual gift of considerable benefit becoming available to you.

Through a combination of wisdom, instinct and intuition, your timing will be excellent and you will not allow anyone or any situation to get the better of you.

A prayer for joy

May all beings know joyful liberation, through mercy, compassion and unconditional divine love. May divine blessings flow in unlimited forms to spiritually benefit all beings. May all beings be eternally happy and free.

SACRED PRACTICE TWO – THE ARISING OF SPRING

The Arising of Spring is a gently stimulating practice fostering light and creativity. This practice is helpful when you feel guided to set intentions and summon the energy necessary to apply yourself in order to manifest something new. It is also nourishing for those times when you want to attract beneficial opportunities and evoke spiritual protection.

Step One – Prepare the Space

How will you establish your sacred space? A simple candle, incense burning or altar could help you channel your focus into inner work, anchoring the intention to step beyond ordinary reality into the liminal spiritual energies that are with us always, but that we do not always notice amongst the distractions of daily life.

Colours that resonate well for spring are green and orange but please be guided by your own sense of what you need. You may like to work with yellow and pink as the colours represented by the deity that you will have the option to invoke in this practice.

Step Two – Prepare Body and Mind

Ground yourself by becoming aware of your body — the weight of your body and the flow of your breath. Choose to be present. Connect to your heart in the way that suits you, perhaps by placing a hand at your heart and reflecting on that which evokes gratitude.

Allow that feeling of gratitude to awaken the energies within your heart. Imagine that the heart is shining with radiant pure love, in all directions. Relax and allow that love to wash through your being, cleansing your body and mind with peaceful, positive energy.

Step Three – Set Intention and Make a Dedication

Do you have a specific intention for the practice? Or are you simply open to what can be revealed through the practice? If you set a specific intention, maintain flexibility in your heart to embrace experiences that may change your way of seeing

your situation. Sometimes we discover that what we thought was the problem is only a symptom and there is a more effective way to manifest a solution.

When you are ready, you can dedicate the practice by declaring, "May spiritual benefit for all beings be authentically generated through this work." This dedication ensures that your practice amplifies the positive and will enhance the benefits of the practice for you and for others indirectly also.

Step Four – Cast the Medicine Circle

The medicine circle is the sacred space within which healing and energy work can safely unfold without distortion or disruption.

Visualise and/or feel that there is pure divine love, shining as a vibrant red jewel, glowing in your heart and sparkling with golden light. That jewel emanates golden-red light in all directions and through all dimensions, forming a subtle energy circle around you. This demarcates the sacred space.

Sense that at each of the four points of the circle—north, south, east and west—as well as above you and below you, there is a strong glowing golden light. This represents the enlightened guardians protecting the circle.

Step Five – Heart of the Practice

Imagine and intend that you are entering into the sacred space within your heart.

In the open spaciousness within your heart, you can sense the vastness of a tree-lined field of wild green grasses, gently bathed in warm golden sunlight. There is spaciousness, aliveness and peace.

Here you can allow yourself to breathe in the cleansing green colours of the wild grasses and allow the healing energies to circulate through your body and mind. Then you can exhale and relax. Repeat the process as you wish.

If you choose to include a deity practice, you can now invoke the solar goddess of light and protection, Marici, with this simple mantra, asking for her support and blessing for your process. As you sound the mantra, imagine a golden pink light glowing in your heart, and warm golden sunlight bathing you from above. These inner and outer lights fill you with creative energy and spiritual protection.

Om Marici Moom Swaha (sounds like OM MA-RITZ-ZAY MOOM SWA-HA)

Step Six – Return

Sense that your process is now complete and you are at the transitionary threshold, ready to return to this moment renewed.

Your inner shift may be radical or subtle but you are ready to step back into your life in a new way. Whatever has arisen for you is what is most needed in this moment. Trust your own soul process.

Step Seven – Closing and Grounding

Slowly move your hands into prayer position at your heart, intending to seal all that has transpired with love. Then say, "It is done."

Intend to bring your awareness completely into the present moment. Sense the air on your skin and the weight of your body in this world. The divine portal closes and all energies from the work dissolve into light and are released to where they can do the most good.

Intend to ground yourself fully in the present moment with some gentle movement.

You have completed your practice.

To succeed, we must know that success is possible … and then believe in ourselves and in the community of guides, guardians, spiritual and earthly helpers that support (and also benefit from) the successful progress of the soul's journey.

When you realise you can work with any experience in a positive way, a fearless quality arises within and you become willing to be you—more freely, more wildly, more joyfully. How the world needs such joy!

Your effort shall bear bountiful, blessed fruit,
beyond your current expectations.

Rest when needed but refuse to turn away from your goal out of fear or fatigue. Let love be your motivation and your fuel.

Acknowledge how far you have come and you will gain confidence in your capabilities. Trust the inner urge to venture forth towards your heart's calling.

*Our Medicine Mother exhibits a benevolent and loving intelligence.
She has gifted you with a precious body and life path for your soul to experience
spiritual growth, awakening and creative play. You can trust in this.*

What your heart seeks is within reach. Do not give up.

Strength and determination to persevere will attract divine blessings of remarkable grace, providing transformation and triumph over all odds.

Be inspired and motivated by love and you will stay the course where others may turn back out of fear.

Turn your mind towards your heart, processing and releasing allegiance to the past, as you ready yourself for a blessed breakthrough.

Playfully welcome the spiritual light with joy in your heart.
Nourish your heart with beauty and spirit.

The beauty of spiritual light can refresh your heart with a compelling reminder of why you are on this path and what you are in the process of manifesting through your sacred work.

Return to your spiritual roots to ground yourself, anchoring your mind to your heart. Here you will find presence, peace and reassurance that there is a loving plan at play, and with your patient persistence, chaos will soon settle into a loving higher order.

Disruption can be rendered divine when we are able to respond to it from a soul level, utilising the dismantling of comfort as a call to evolve into a new and more conscious way of life.

As you plant your spiritual roots deeply, you can feel supported even during times of upheaval and transformation, recognising these as temporary symptoms of spiritual growth and progress.

Earth Mother constantly demonstrates the reality of unity within apparent diversity. Take care not to pigeonhole your soul. Embrace all facets of your vast multidimensional being.

SACRED PRACTICE THREE – THE VIBRANCY OF SUMMER

The Vibrancy of Summer is a spiritual practice to heighten your confidence in shining your light, and having the courage to live your truth. It can be utilised during the high-energy, demanding times of your life to keep the spark alive (until it is time for you to rest) or to evoke the feeling of lightness and brightness when encountering a challenging phase.

Step One – Prepare the Space

How will you establish your sacred space? A simple candle, incense burning or altar could help you channel your focus into inner work, anchoring the intention to step beyond ordinary reality into the liminal spiritual energies that are with us always, but that we do not always notice amongst the distractions of daily life.

Colours that resonate well for summer are red and pink, but please be guided by your own sense of what you need. You may prefer to work with other colours such as gold and yellow that represent the solar energy or blue and white to represent soft clouds in a bright summer sky.

Step Two – Prepare Body and Mind

Ground yourself by becoming aware of your body — the weight of your body and the flow of your breath. Choose to be present. Connect to your heart in the way that suits you, perhaps by placing a hand at your heart and reflecting on that which evokes gratitude.

Allow that feeling of gratitude to awaken the energies within your heart. Imagine that the heart is shining with radiant pure love, in all directions. Relax and allow that love to wash through your being, cleansing your body and mind with peaceful, positive energy.

Step Three – Set Intention and Make a Dedication

Do you have a specific intention for the practice? Or are you simply open to what can be revealed through the practice? If you set a specific intention, maintain flexibility in your heart to embrace experiences that may change your way of seeing your situation. Sometimes we discover that what we thought was the problem is only a symptom and there is a more effective way to manifest a solution.

When you are ready, you can dedicate the practice by declaring, "May spiritual benefit for all beings be authentically generated through this work." This dedication ensures that your practice amplifies the positive and will enhance the benefits of the practice for you and for others indirectly also.

Step Four – Cast the Medicine Circle

The medicine circle is the sacred space within which healing and energy work can safely unfold without distortion or disruption.

Visualise and/or feel that there is pure divine love, shining as a vibrant red jewel, glowing in your heart and sparkling with golden light. That jewel emanates golden-red light in all directions and through all dimensions, forming a subtle energy circle around you. This demarcates the sacred space.

Sense that at each of the four points of the circle—north, south, east and west—as well as above you and below you, there is a strong glowing golden light. This represents the enlightened guardians protecting the circle.

Step Five – Heart of the Practice

Imagine and intend that you are entering into the sacred space within your heart.

In the vastness of that open spaciousness within your heart, you can sense a pleasant warmth in the air, and a feeling of wellbeing and relaxation pervades the atmosphere. There may be the buzz of bees or the singing of birds in the distance, and perhaps you are resting under the shade of a tree or basking in the radiant sunlight.

Here you can revitalise yourself, body and mind, allowing your energies to be topped up by the happiness and vitality pulsating through the spiritual environment. Sense your inner subtle fire glowing and sparking joyfully. Sense your heart warm and happy and relaxed. Breathe in and out. Sense the abundant radiant energies readily available to you now.

If you wish to include a deity practice, you can now invoke the protective goddess Red Tara who amplifies magnetic attraction of positive energy and tames negativities. With this simple mantra, you are asking for her support and blessing for your process. As you sound the mantra, imagine a warm glowing red light shining bright within your heart. Positive energies radiate in all directions and into all dimensions from this bright light. Sense your own energy becoming more positive and joyful.

Om Tare Tam Swaha (sounds like OM TAR-RAY TUM SWA-HA)

Step Six – Return

Sense that your process is now complete and you are at the transitionary threshold, ready to return to this moment renewed.

Your inner shift may be radical or subtle but you are ready to step back into your life in a new way. Whatever has arisen for you is what is most needed in this moment. Trust your own soul process.

Step Seven – Closing and Grounding

Slowly move your hands into prayer position at your heart, intending to seal all that has transpired with love. Then say, "It is done."

Intend to bring your awareness completely into the present moment. Sense the air on your skin and the weight of your body in this world. The divine portal closes and all energies from the work dissolve into light and are released to where they can do the most good.

Intend to ground yourself fully in the present moment with some gentle movement.

You have completed your practice.

Your openness is precious, and so you are guided to discern between that which nourishes and is wise to allow to flow, and that which needs to be clamped and cut off. Express your boundaries with wisdom.

Spiritual maturity can have the effect of strengthening and stimulating our capacity for sacred refusal. Sometimes 'no' is a divine word of blessing, protecting both the prospective enabler and enabled from sabotaging themselves.

Affirm your right to secure the sanctity of your soul and the integrity of your energy.

Shamans of the Tuva region in southern Siberia are known to focus less on psychic protection and more on becoming filled with blessings from the spirits. You have it within you to embrace this joyful way to say 'yes' and 'no' all at once.

Swap your allegiance to appearances for a deeper faith in yourself and the divine mandate that your higher purpose needs to manifest in our world—and therefore will be supported.

Believe that even the greatest apparent obstacle is a hidden helping hand, teaching your soul how to become strong enough to accomplish your authentic purpose.

A prayer to the Divine Mother Tree

With greatest respect, I summon the Divine Mother Tree Tara, who loves all beings unconditionally, and serves the primordial wisdom of liberation, peace, love and truth. May your will and wisdom manifest now. May this healing occur for the spiritual benefit of all beings.

Wilkins

Hold yourself accountable but treat yourself with compassion and kindness, too. Focus on continuing to grow as you recognise how far you have already come.

As you explore your ancestral inheritances, you will discern between that which needs containment in a strong boundary and that which can be openly received. You will find and claim the goodness hiding in your history for your own soul's empowerment.

Your sacred path will at times call for periods of solitude when disturbing activities should not take place. This is not escapism, but a time of replenishment and preparation for the next steps on your authentic and inspired life path.

Give your process the time it needs.

As the colour of blood and life, red expresses life-enhancing magic to overpower destructive energies with life-honouring, affirmative spiritual power. You can accentuate the positive—not as a way of ignoring the negative—but as a means of establishing a position of enhanced spiritual strength from which you can proceed with wisdom.

Challenges that you are working through are purposeful, divine catalysts for your healing and transformation.

Your transformational journey into empowerment will include twists and turns as you move through the depths of your darkness and the ecstasy of your light, shedding resistance, realising wisdom, and embracing life with a fearless heart.

Love yourself by intuitively differentiating between divine disruption that you can work with creatively for personal growth, and unproductive, chaotic disturbance which requires a strong boundary.

To find purpose in the struggle is one way that we surrender to the path without losing our sense of spiritual empowerment. We recognise the struggles as the mysteries that will reveal their secret grace in time.

Wilkins

SACRED PRACTICE FOUR – THE HARVEST OF AUTUMN

The Harvest of Autumn is a practice that supports the finalising of a cycle or experience, allowing you to fully process, distil the wisdom and integrate the blessings. This is a practice to enhance spiritual metabolism and digestion. You can utilise this practice at any time you need to make sense of something or integrate an experience.

Step One – Prepare the Space

How will you establish your sacred space? A simple candle, incense burning or altar could help you channel your focus into inner work, anchoring the intention to step beyond ordinary reality into the liminal spiritual energies that are with us always, but that we do not always notice amongst the distractions of daily life.

Colours that resonate well for autumn are red and purple, orange and blue, but please be guided by your own sense of what you need. You may prefer to work with cool or warm colours based on your intuitive sense of what you need in the moment.

Step Two – Prepare Body and Mind

Ground yourself by becoming aware of your body — the weight of your body and the flow of your breath. Choose to be present. Connect to your heart in the way that suits you, perhaps by placing a hand at your heart and reflecting on that which evokes gratitude.

Allow that feeling of gratitude to awaken the energies within your heart. Imagine that the heart is shining with radiant pure love, in all directions. Relax and allow that love to wash through your being, cleansing your body and mind with peaceful, positive energy.

Step Three – Set Intention and Make a Dedication

Do you have a specific intention for the practice? Or are you simply open to what can be revealed through the practice? If you set a specific intention, maintain flexibility in your heart to embrace experiences that may change your way of seeing

your situation. Sometimes we discover that what we thought was the problem is only a symptom and there is a more effective way to manifest a solution.

When you are ready, you can dedicate the practice by declaring, "May spiritual benefit for all beings be authentically generated through this work." This dedication ensures that your practice amplifies the positive and will enhance the benefits of the practice for you and for others indirectly also.

Step Four – Cast the Medicine Circle

The medicine circle is the sacred space within which healing and energy work can safely unfold without distortion or disruption.

Visualise and/or feel that there is pure divine love, shining as a vibrant red jewel, glowing in your heart and sparkling with golden light. That jewel emanates golden-red light in all directions and through all dimensions, forming a subtle energy circle around you. This demarcates the sacred space.

Sense that at each of the four points of the circle—north, south, east and west—as well as above you and below you, there is a strong glowing golden light. This represents the enlightened guardians protecting the circle.

Step Five – Heart of the Practice

Imagine and intend that you are entering into the sacred space within your heart.

In the vastness of that open spaciousness within your heart, you can sense a seemingly endless clear blue sky above you. The air is crisp and the light is flawless and clear. Beneath you are an abundance of crunchy, bright red and orange fallen leaves. There is a feeling of vibrancy and fruition — also completion and fulfilment.

Here you can allow for a winnowing through your soul as the spiritual breath of life flows through your soul like a soft autumn breeze. This breath of life effortlessly loosens the husks from the precious spiritual grains … sense the release of the superfluous and the gathering of the precious golden grains as seeds of light, dissolving into your heart.

If you wish to include a deity practice, you can now invoke the goddess and queen of two worlds, Persephone, with this simple prayer asking for her support and blessing for your process. As you sound the words, imagine a golden energy that has dissolved into your heart, nurturing and enriching all facets of your being.

Persephone, Daughter of Demeter, Proserpine, Kore, descend and arise in my heart, Abundant Queen of Life (sounds like PUR-SEF-FOE-NEE, Daughter of DEE-MEE-TUR, PRO-SUR-PEE-NAH, KOR-RAY).

Step Six – Return

Sense that your process is now complete and you are at the transitionary threshold, ready to return to this moment renewed.

Your inner shift may be radical or subtle but you are ready to step back into your life in a new way. Whatever has arisen for you is what is most needed in this moment. Trust your own soul process.

Step Seven – Closing and Grounding

Slowly move your hands into prayer position at your heart, intending to seal all that has transpired with love. Then say, "It is done."

Intend to bring your awareness completely into the present moment. Sense the air on your skin and the weight of your body in this world. The divine portal closes and all energies from the work dissolve into light and are released to where they can do the most good.

Intend to ground yourself fully in the present moment with some gentle movement.

You have completed your practice.

A shamanic soul must find the courage to stand upon one's inner spiritual ground. By refusing to cave to self-doubt, the soul becomes strong and sacredness can shine as a subtle radiance from within.

There is a sacred, primal need for the shamanic soul to outgrow convention, to overcome the fear that bonds one to externally-driven value systems, and to live from the inner values of the heart.

The shamanic soul yearns for expansion and depth, beyond safely sanctioned society, from a place of personal integrity and truth.

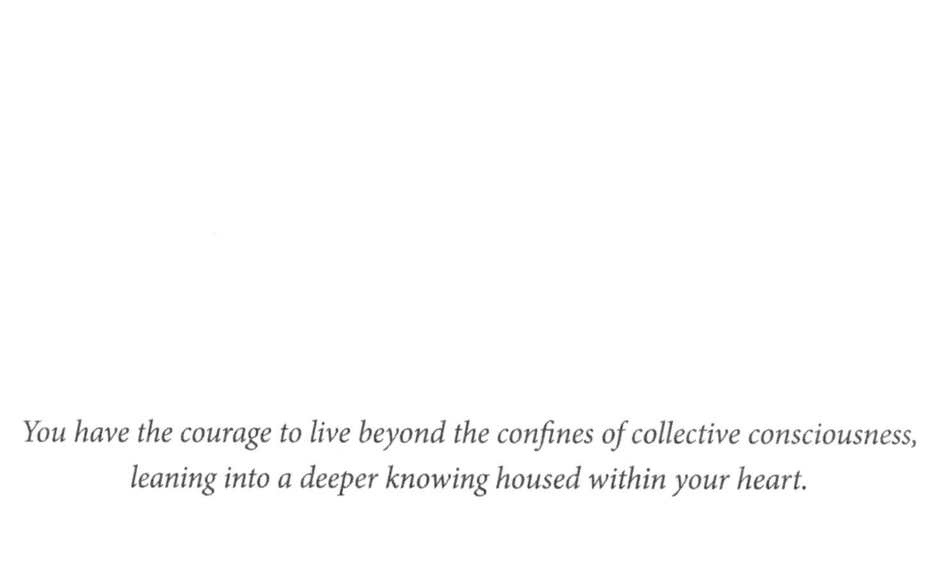

You have the courage to live beyond the confines of collective consciousness, leaning into a deeper knowing housed within your heart.

Your guardianship of the sacred in your life is an expression of spiritual respect and reverence, which generates far-reaching benefit for humanity and our planet.

Your heart can be light and free, and yet care deeply and radiate compassion for all beings. To lighten the heart is to learn that we are worthy — of love, of peace, of respect, of care. Rather than demanding that the world provide this for us, we learn to give this to ourselves. We develop the capacity for self-love.

A prayer for Protection

With the greatest reverence, I call upon Our Lady Isis, our Divine Mother of love, wisdom, magic and spiritual protection. I call upon the wisdom and power of your buckle, belt and knot. Radiant one in possession of higher knowledge and navigational skill, knowing when and how to deny, and when and how to permit. You are the power of intention, courage and word. I ask for your protection and assistance, so that my empowerment may generate spiritual benefit for all.

LIBER

Neither caterpillar nor chrysalis ways will work for the emerging butterfly. Nature demonstrates the courage needed to abandon oneself into the miraculous realm of transformation. And at the opportune moment, you will be ready to claim your wings.

Befriend yourself and your heart will naturally open to attract and enjoy the divine warmth that desires entry into your world.

Wisdom will protect you from enabling destructive behaviour and compassion will generate unconditional regard within your heart, freeing you to live and let live.

Healing the divine masculine energy within helps the soul become ready to stand up for its own light and be willing to do what it takes to live its truth and uniqueness.

Turn to the light within your heart as a place of sanctuary, kindness, unconditional support and true friendliness with yourself. Know that all is not lost, and that love is the most powerful, enduring and healing presence in all of existence.

Sense the sacred friendship that exists between the divine heart and yours.

Keep your heart hopeful, for love will always find a way.